Screw The Joneses

Screw The Joneses

✦

27 1/2 Tips on How to Have a Blast While You Last

Kristy Frances

iUniverse, Inc.

New York Lincoln Shanghai

Screw The Joneses
27 1/2 Tips on How to Have a Blast While You Last

iUniverse books may be ordered through booksellers or by contacting:

iUniverse
2021 Pine Lake Road, Suite 100
Lincoln, NE 68512
www.iuniverse.com
1-800-Authors (1-800-288-4677)

Because of the dynamic nature of the Internet, any Web addresses or links contained in this book may have changed since publication and may no longer be valid.

The views expressed in this work are solely those of the author and do not necessarily reflect the views of the publisher, and the publisher hereby disclaims any responsibility for them.

ISBN: 978-0-595-46548-4 (pbk)
ISBN: 978-0-595-90843-1 (ebk)

Printed in the United States of America

Acknowledgments

There are so many wonderful people that have contributed to this work in my life—and for them, I am thankful. But I am most grateful to the ones who inspired me to write this book:

Mr. and Mrs. Jones!

Contents

Material possessions

Relationships

On experiences

The American Way!

♦

Mom, baseball, apple pie.... The Joneses!

Who are these Joneses anyway and why are they so important to us?

The Joneses are, hypothetically, the people next door—who have it all! Oops! What I really mean is that we *think* they have it all. They are happy, healthy, wealthy, have perfect spouses and perfect children. No wonder we have to keep up with the Joneses. We want what they have! We want it so desperately that we are willing to risk too much.

The Joneses have presented to us some unique challenges. Although this challenge is omnipresent in our lives, it often goes unspoken. Our kids absolutely must have the latest and greatest scooter, just like little Johnny Jones next door. Or, Mom must have that new, decked-out mini van that Joan Jones just drove into the driveway. How about Dad, coveting that shiny, brand new rider mower that John Jones rides, grinning proudly as he drives by every single Saturday morning?

Never mind the new boat, the beautiful landscaping, Olympic sized pool, the best clothes money can buy. All at what price? The answer is quite simple: at the price of our *sanity*!

Why is it that we must keep up with the Joneses? Why is that drive so strong that it gnaws away at our very being? "If they can have it, so must I!" It is so important to us that we "appear" to be financially well off. If we can keep up with the Joneses, who are doing so well financially, then we too must be well off—or at least the Joneses think we are. Success! We achieved the goal—Mr. Jones (and everyone else) thinks I'm equally as well off as him!

Meanwhile, our credit card bills are soaring sky high (along with those great interest rates), our checks are bouncing like rubber balls and our second mortgages have become impossible to pay. We are up to our eyeballs in debt and on the verge of a heart attack! Sound familiar?

Screw the Joneses! Get your life back! Read on to learn just how …

Prologue

I married the videographer

It would be really a juicy story if I said that I left the groom standing at the altar and married the videographer instead—but then I wouldn't be telling the truth.

I asked Michael (the videographer) if he would film my wedding because he had made a beautiful video of my sister's wedding. He said to me, "Of course, but when the priest asks if anyone objects, I'll be the first to raise my hand!" Out of curiosity, I asked the inevitable question, "Why would you do that?" He responded, "Because I haven't had a chance to date you yet!" I told him he was nuts and that there would never, ever be an opportunity for us to be together because #1) I was crazy-in-love with my wealthy fiancé, and #2) I was not interested in dating him.

Fourteen months later, Michael and I were married.

Three months before my original wedding, I accepted the fact that my fiancé was an alcoholic. I had to make the decision that I could not live my life with that disease, so we called the wedding off. Michael and I were good friends at the time. We attended the same church and belonged to a fantastic young adults group. We became best friends and have been the best of friends since then. This union was the prelude to my lifelong journey of a very strong "Screw the Joneses" mentality. I just didn't know it at the time.

"True happiness is being married to your best friend"

~Unknown

Financial Crises

We had it all! We had a nice house, new cars and a boat, but along with that came mortgages and loans. We were "keeping up with the Joneses", No Problem! I was blessed because I was a stay-at-home mom. Michael worked hard so we could have "the life".

One day, everything changed. While installing a two hundred pound window, Michael turned the wrong way and broke his back. He was no longer able to work and our income came to a rapid halt. We immediately put the house up for sale. Months earlier I had put all my efforts into starting a home based business, but there was no way that my little income could support our monthly bills.

When the house wouldn't sell, we took a second mortgage out to pay the first and maxed out our credit cards to survive. We stole from Peter to pay Paul. Prozac kept me going.

Finally the house sold and we moved to Michael's vacant family farm house in Pennsylvania. I found a wonderful job and Michael stayed at home with our daughter, Maranda, while he rested his back.

I was only twenty eight at the time, and I am SO THANKFUL for that challenging experience. Now, while still very young, we are able to apply these hard-earned lessons to our lives, and hopefully share these experiences with others!

"I don't measure a man's success by how high he climbs but how high he bounces when he hits bottom."

~General George S. Patton

Lessons Learned

- Life is short
- You may not always have your health
- Don't wait until retirement to begin living life
- A little debt is ok—a lot of debt stinks
- Live life Simply—do more with less
- Live your life for you—and your family—not the Joneses!

This short book will share these lessons with some recommendations on what we believe truly works …

27½ Tips on How to
Have a Blast While You Last

I. Material possessions

II. Relationships

III. Life experiences

Material possessions

Tip # 1

Buy a comfortable, practical home

Buy a home you can afford with low payments so you don't run out of money before you run out of month. Also, make sure the home has low maintenance so you have time to play.

I was appalled when I first heard the term "house poor". We were celebrating Thanksgiving at my sister's house when a newly married couple, Ron and Jane, shared their story with us. They each had jobs with very long hours, trying to make ends meet. Ron said, "We got married last year and bought a beautiful new home (as most new married couples do). It's sad because we work such long hours that we are not home long enough to enjoy it. When we aren't working our jobs, we're working on the house. We are 'house poor'. Our mortgage is so high, that almost all of our income goes to paying for the house. We don't have much left over to do anything extra."

I wanted to cry! Everything I believed in came into focus as Ron shared with me his very personal challenge.

Many families decide to build their lives around their homes and that is great, for them. We believe that if you are the Joneses, and have a lot of money, by all means, have that big beautiful home, but hire lots of people to take care of it for you so you have time to play!

When we had a home with land and a huge mortgage, Michael worked hard all week long. I spent many hours a day preparing meals, managing finances, cooking, cleaning and caring for Maranda. Our "free time" consisted of mowing the yard, pruning the trees, maintaining the pool, cleaning and maintaining the house (we had a huge "honey do" list.) It seemed like we had no time for fun.

Michael and I now believe that a home is very important and that there are three ingredients that a home must have in order for us to be happy ... a house is simply a place to 1) feel secure 2) spend quality time with family 3) sleep.

So we bought a twelve hundred square foot condo in a safe neighborhood and fantastic school district. We are on the first floor and have a nature preserve in our backyard for Maranda to explore. I could pay the mortgage if I worked a minimum wage job—full time. We have minimal maintenance.

Michael and I choose to live in a very comfortable home, but below our means, so that we can use the extra money for other things. Keep reading!

Why is it that people wait until they are sixty to decide they want to live simply, in a condo, so they can enjoy life?

"*A man is a success if he gets up in the morning and gets to bed at night, and in between he does what he wants to do*".

~*Bob Dylan*

Tip # 2

Buy beautiful used cars

Why is it that people buy new cars even though they know that it loses about $5,000 in value when they drive it off the lot?

If you have the last name Jones, this will work for you just fine.

If not, what are you thinking? Who cares (other than the Joneses) if you have a brand new car?

Michael and I looked at three options when shopping for a car: buying new, leasing, or buying used. Hands down, we decided on buying beautiful, used cars. We buy them about two years old, with less than 35,000 miles, for less than $10,000 (preferably cash). And, yes we have the cash because we live below our means. Interest stinks and it will suck you dry!

This way, we have *no car payments*! We have fun cars that look great. A car needs to get you safely from here to there. Why spend $30,000 when you can pay $10,000 and spend the difference on traveling and having fun? Or, you can do like we did and save the difference in a special account and buy a beautiful, used motorcycle.

"A table, a chair, a bowl of fruit and a violin; what else does a man need to be happy?"

~Albert Einstein

Tip # 3

Buy first what you need and then what you want

How many times have you and your spouse gone shopping and said this to each other: "This _____would be great for when we have guests over!"

YUK!

Now, put on the "Screw the Joneses hat" and look around your home and say to yourself, "What do I really need?"

Return all the things you don't need to the store and get your money back. You can probably afford a fantastic vacation (or make a contribution to your child's college fund)!

I realize this is way overboard, but the lesson is that we are overly concerned about what people think when they visit our homes! Why? Because we are judged by the home that we keep, the vehicles that we drive, and the "things" that we have. Unfortunately, this is reality! And the Joneses have set the pace!

Michael and I made a lot of money over the last three years and we still appear to be "middle" class. For many years we made an average salary. We had a basic condo, used cars and few material "things". Our income tripled over the past three years, but you could *never* tell by looking at our lifestyle. We could have easily bought a bigger home and filled it with expensive china, high tech televisions and name brand furniture. But, we didn't want to increase our overhead, so we decided instead to live below our means and put the extra money into smart places. We used the money for travel, retirement, investments and our daughter's college fund—much more meaningful "things" that can't be seen!

"*Things*" are not important to us, but "*life experiences*" are!

When our friends come to visit, they don't judge. They appreciate our freedom and individuality! (I'll bet some wish they had the guts to do the same!)

What would your life be like if you didn't care how people "classified" you when they saw your home, your cars and your things? You should try it some time! What a relief!

"Our ultimate freedom is the right and power to decide how anybody or anything outside ourselves will affect us."

~Stephen R. Covey

Relationships

Tip # 4

Kids should be a welcome addition to your marriage

Agree to be a union first and let the kids join your union. (Moms—please pay very close attention to this!)

According to an article in the New York Times, almost fifty percent of all marriages in America end in divorce. A very large percentage of them are somehow related to this tip! If we can get this step down, there would be much more happiness and much less divorce! Michael taught me this priceless lesson because he was an unlucky statistic of this age-old problem. Unfortunately for him, it contributed to the demise of his first marriage. Fortunately for me, our family is stronger and happier. Michael helped me to see this when I was pregnant with Maranda. We made an agreement to be a solid union first and then welcome her to that union.

It is a *natural tendency* for women to have babies and then allow them to become the center of their worlds. It is so amazing to have a baby grow inside of you and then bring it into the world. It is so very easy to give the baby all of your love and attention. I have seen it a hundred times! I am certain that I would have made the same mistake, had it not been for Michael's experience. Children do demand a lot of our time and energy, and we can't help but love them to pieces. However, it is up to us to dictate the timing and energy.

A man and woman get married and agree to become *one*. Their union must be a strong, unbreakable foundation for their future family. As children are added to this union, they become the building blocks that are added on top of the foundation. If the children maneuver their way into the existing foundation, the building (or family) crumbles. Often, parents allow the children to come in between their marriage, therefore resulting in divorce.

What am I talking about?

Do you kiss your spouse when he walks in the door?

Do you date your spouse? (Yes, get a babysitter, the child will be just fine! Make this sacrifice now and your child will ultimately be even happier!)

Do you "work" at keeping your marriage alive?

Do you put your children to bed early enough so you can spend quality time with your spouse? (You dictate bedtime—not them).

Do you agree on things before you answer your children, so that your children see you as one and don't "work one against the other"?

If you disagree about a message your spouse is delivering to your children, do you handle it behind closed doors and not in front of them?

Do your children see the affection and attention you give each other?

Do they know their place (spouse #1 and children #2)?

Do your children feel secure in your marriage?

Do you know how important it is to stay healthy and in shape so that you maintain the beautiful person that your spouse married?

I have met people (mostly men) who admit that they feel invisible when they go home. Often they come home from a hard day's work and open the front door to a nagging wife (who also had a hard day). Although the home is filled with family members, they feel empty inside. To avoid the pain, many men choose to work extra hours and finally go home when everyone in the house is sleeping.

The good news is—it's not too late to make this agreement yourself! It takes work, but the result is a strong foundation on which to build an impenetrable, strong and happy family!

"The kindest thing a father can do for their children is to love their mother."

~Unknown

Tip # 5

Show your kids the world

Remember in tip number three, where I wrote about limiting material possessions, saving money and living below your means? If you follow that step, you are well on your way to "Showing your kids the world"!

Have you ever tried to take your kid out of school for a week to go to Washington DC? Nine times out of ten, the teacher will say, "That's great! Your child will learn more there than they will in class this next week!"

We can proudly say that Maranda visited twenty five states and two countries before she turned ten! We firmly believe in traveling (with our daughter and sometimes without!)

One summer, Maranda and I took a road trip. I took one week off of work. We bought loads of junk food, packed bunches of CDs, and we sang and ate our way to Busch Gardens. We spent two days in Tampa and then learned that Hurricane Charlie was coming our way. We spent the rest of our trip running away from Charlie. We had so much fun charting the course!

I'll never forget going to a silly magnet shop in Downtown Disney where we bought Flarp (it's like blubber in a can). When you take out the blubber and push it back into the can, it makes a gaseous sound. We went into a nice restaurant and hid in the bathroom. We made funny sounds and laughed our hearts out! I left the stall and washed my hands. The faces and gestures I witnessed outside the noisy stall were unforgettable! (Ok, Bad Mommy! That's okay because it's worth the memory to me!)

When Maranda went back to school that fall and was asked what she did during the summer, what do you think she enjoyed talking about? She will continue to talk about the Flarp experience to this day. In addition, her teachers always tell me how much they enjoy her participation in all class discussions. She has had so many experiences and has a lot to share: from lilacs, to geysers, to lobsters, to Reggae music!

Also, if you ask her today about her favorite memories growing up, the answers are always about the great experiences she had while traveling. It's what memories are made of. CREATE MEMORIES WITH YOUR KIDS—NOW! DON'T WAIT UNTIL YOU HAVE A LOT OF MONEY—IT MAY NEVER HAPPEN! CAMPING AND ROADTRIPS ARE CHEAP!

"Life is not measured by the number of breaths we take, but by the moments that take our breath away"
~Unknown

Tip # 6

Be your spouse's LIFE PARTNER

I believe that being a partner to your spouse is the first step to achieving a successful marriage. If couples look at marriage as a partnership, as playing on the same team, life can throw them all kinds of punches but never knock them out! Too many couples are on opposing teams. There is one leader—but no follower. Even worse, the husband is going in one direction while the wife goes in another. Often, the Joneses are so focused on success at work that they forget about the success of the vital partnership at home! This is not Milton Bradley's Game of LIFE—*it is life*! Choose your partner wisely and form a team that cannot be beaten. Who makes the calls? That's up to you. Just make sure the receiving party is aware of the play and is successful at making the play. Are you a Life Partner to your spouse?

"Love is composed of a single soul inhabiting two bodies".

~Aristotle

Tip # 7

Communicate with your spouse

Communication is *always* an issue in *every* relationship. There have been millions of books written on the subject.

First and foremost: every word that comes out of our mouths needs to be truthful. If that happens and we can be trusted, good communication becomes more successful. Michael set me straight when we first started dating. He told me, "Don't ever lie to me. If you do, you will lose all of my trust in you." That was a very powerful statement. Imagine losing all trust just because of one lie! I think we should all live by this rule. Imagine how much easier life would be!

When Michael and I were having our challenges, we met with a counselor. We learned a magnificent lesson and I share this with my friends to this day.

When people tell you something and it hurts you, or if you don't understand the message, tell them, "Here is what I understand you are saying to me". In your own words repeat back to them the message as you interpreted it. Often, the intent of the message was misinterpreted. It could be the choice of words and the order they were given or it could be the volume of the voice. How many times have you said something and then ended up saying "I didn't mean it that way!" This practice offers the opportunity to make sure that the message was received correctly.

Another important skill to master for successful communication is listening. Everyone has heard the saying, "You have two ears and one mouth. Use them proportionately". We have heard it, but do we practice this message?

I say no. I am very guilty myself. Michael says to me constantly, "Quit thinking about what you are going to say next and LISTEN to what I am saying now." Many of us do this. We are already thinking about how we are going to respond to something before the complete message is delivered. Therefore, we miss parts of the message. If we can teach ourselves to be better listeners—and learn how to turn off our inner voices when someone is speaking to us—we can communicate better!

Communication is key to a relationship. This is something we need to work on improving every day.

"I like to listen. I have learned a great deal from listening carefully. Most people never listen."

~Ernest Hemingway

Tip # 8

Be your spouse's "biggest fan"

As a child, it is our parents who are our biggest fans. They watched us on the football field or on stage and shouted our names. They were so proud of us and told us that "You can do it". But as we grow up and get married, our spouse needs to step into those shoes. Our spouse should be our biggest fan. In turn, we need to be our spouse's biggest fan. Be the wind beneath his wings. Help him to reach for the stars and be the best he can be. Why, because both husband and wife will soar together. What a great place to be!

"My most brilliant achievement was my ability to be able to persuade my wife to marry me."

~Winston Churchill

Tip # 9

Put your spouse on a pedestal

I realize this may sound silly—but it is the best way that I can describe how important it is to honor your spouse. If you can truly put your spouse on a pedestal and treat him like royalty, he will respond in kind. Show him respect and take care of his needs. Treat him with kindness and honor his existence. Tell him how wonderful, gorgeous, and smart he is. If you tell him that he is great, he will feel appreciated and will typically respond in kind. If you feel this way toward your spouse—please tell him. He won't know unless you do! This will really help build his self esteem and will ultimately help him to be the best partner he can possibly be!

"If you cannot inspire a woman with love of you, fill her above the brim with love of herself; all that runs over will be yours."

~Charles Caleb Colton

Tip # 10

Give each other freedom

Of course this statement must be built on trust. Everyone is an individual and must have time to "be who they are" and spend time doing the things they love. Spouses are guilty of holding each other back and not allowing each other to do the things they did prior to marriage. When we get married, it does not mean that we have to leave who we *are* and become someone else. It is so important for spouses to honor each other's individuality and allow them the space and freedom to enjoy what they love to do.

I love to dance with my girlfriends. Michael encourages me to take the time to be with my friends and go dancing. Several of my friends aren't allowed to go because their husband won't let them. What? I'm not being accusatory, but often the husband doesn't trust himself therefore, he imposes that mistrust on his wife.

Whatever Michael wants to do, like go fishing with his guy friends, take a cross-country motorcycle ride, meet friends at a bar or take a boat trip to the Bahamas, I support it. I want him to have time to be himself and do the things he enjoys. I honestly have no problem with it whatsoever. Besides, I usually get lots of extra love and kisses when he returns.

Tip # 11

Be home by Six

I realize this will not apply to everyone—but the point needs to be addressed. Again, I thank my incredible husband (and my Dad) for this very valuable lesson.

I asked my Dad, "Now that you are very experienced at living life, what would you have done differently?" His answer was, "I would have worked much less and would have spent more time with my family!" How many of you would say exactly the same thing?

When Maranda asks me that question on my death bed that will NOT be my answer! In fact, I ask myself that question constantly and adjust my life accordingly so I have no regrets. Know why? Because Michael told me to stop working and be home by six! He reminded me that work wouldn't collapse without me—that it will be there when I go back the next morning. This applies to all of us!

If we move everything from our inbox to our outbox, there will be nothing left to do. It is not possible to finish everything! Work will continue to pile up. And we go to work every day to empty our inboxes. That's just what we do!

Most employers are tuned in to "work/life balance" and will support us in our family life. We just have to ask for it. If they don't, see tip #15 "Love your job or leave".

After Michael and I get home from work, we ask each other "What's for dinner?" We look in the fridge or freezer and find something to cook. I make a fresh salad and we throw together a quick, healthy meal. Michael cooks and Maranda and I clean. I refuse to stress over a silly meal! We typically ignore the phones because that is our family time. We spend the rest of the evening talking about our days, planning for our next vacation, doing homework, etc. Rather than asking our daughter "How was school"? We ask, "Tell me three things I don't know about you or about your day today".

When people are asked on their deathbeds what they would have done differently, the answer has never been, "I wish I had spent more time at the office".

Tip # 12

Marry someone who wants the same things you do ...

Need I say more?

"Love does not consist in gazing at each other, but in looking outward together in the same direction."

~Antoine de Saint-Exupery

Tip # 13

Job opportunities come often, but children are young only once.

I received this excellent advice from a successful, widowed friend of mine.

I had a great job! I was quite successful and gaining the recognition and attention of the executive team. I was climbing that corporate ladder! One day, my phone rang with an incredible, not to be missed, offer: A promotion! More money, more travel, more recognition! Sounds great! But wait a minute. More travel? At what expense?

After digging a little deeper, I learned that the promotion would require traveling forty percent of the time. *(Translation—two nights in a hotel, at least, per week.)*

Who's going to tuck Maranda into bed every night? What about prayer time? Who's going to listen to her each evening as she shares the important experiences and dilemmas that she had that day? What about help with homework, boys and friends? Sure, someone else can fill my role (and Michael would be great at it). But, heck no! I'm not giving that up! My time with my girl is sooo precious, yet sooo short!

My answer to my manager was "No, not now!"

I look at it this way: My work life extends from about age fifteen to age sixty five. That is fifty years of work! My child's most challenging years are from about age eleven to eighteen. That is seven years. Seven out of fifty years is nothing! That is less than fifteen percent of my life that is deducted from "career climbing". I will wait. I choose to wait! I don't need to be the Joneses (or need to keep up with them for that matter). I need to be wife, mommy and me. I'll climb that ladder later. Not now. I have never looked back!

On experiences

Tip # 14

Hire a maid

I despise deep cleaning! I can certainly tidy up and do basic cleaning. But, when it comes to toilets, showers and windows, I'd like to pass!

How? I look at it this way: Do what you do best and earn enough money to have someone do the things you don't like to do. Period!

Our maid comes every other week. She takes care of all the deep cleaning so that I don't have to stress over it. I'll work harder at what I love to do and earn enough money to pay her.

Tip # 14 1/2

Ask your neighbor (Mrs. Jones) for a reference! I'm sure she knows someone great.

Tip # 15

Love your job or leave

If you don't wake up in the morning excited about work, then go back to sleep! Keep hitting the snooze button until you are ready to wake up. Wake up, shower, get dressed, go to your computer and write a resignation letter. Take it to your boss, put in your two weeks, and leave!

Again, I know this is strong, but I mean it! I did it myself! I was in a sales job where I was not satisfied with the delivery of the service. I would get a contract, turn it over to the delivery team to service the contract, and time and time again, they dropped the ball! The excuses were endless. But, to me, if my client wasn't completely satisfied, that was unacceptable.

I decided that I can't work a job like that because I can't sell something that I don't believe in. I was very patient and offered to help any way I could, but it didn't seem to get any better. I found that I wasn't "springing" out of bed like I normally did. I actually got to the point where I was dragging myself to work. I was very unhappy there. I shared this with Michael and he told me to quit. Remember, we live below our means, so we can do these risky things. What freedom!

Several of my coworkers (with big homes and new cars) were so envious of me! They asked, "How can you do that? How can you just quit?" I explained that I wasn't happy and that I had to do something every day that energized me—not sucked the life out of me! Yes, I can make that choice because *I can*! So, here I sit writing this crazy book because I'm not at my life-sucking job.

I'll find something else I really love to do and get paid to do it! If you have the guts to take a chance on loving what you do every day—take the plunge! It's worth it! Why would you spend fifty percent of your "awake" time doing something you don't like to do? Funny how we get "stuck" in our lives.

"To business that we love, we rise betime and go to 't with delight."

~William Shakespeare

Tip # 16

Live before you die

Bill and Sue were our next door neighbors. Bill was an auto mechanic and Sue was a nurse. They worked hard at their jobs for many years. They were so excited because they were finally able to retire at the age of sixty five. They worked to save up for a beautiful camper so they could enjoy retirement and explore the world.

Bill and Sue spent so much of their lives working toward retirement; they forgot to have fun in the meantime. I would ask them why they didn't take time to travel and they would respond that they were "saving up for their retirement!" Lo and behold, they set off on day number one in their beautiful new camper and Sue had a heart attack and died. I can't tell you how many times I have heard similar stories. This makes me so sad. I refuse to let this happen to us. Yes, I will "save" for our retirement, but I will "spend" now. I can't take money to my grave!

One day, I pulled my cute (debt free) car into a fruit stand along a busy highway. The strawberries were fresh and I couldn't resist! As I was paying for my small treasure, the clerk said to me, "When I retire, I'm going to buy a convertible car and dye my hair blonde—just like you!" I responded, "Lady, what are you waiting for?" Reality is, anything could happen between now and when she retires. There is no guarantee that if she waits until she retires, she will be around to enjoy it!

"Twenty years from now you will be more disappointed by the things that you didn't do than by the ones you did do. So throw off the bowlines. Sail away from the safe harbor. Catch the trade winds in your sails. Explore. Dream. Discover."

~Mark Twain

Tip # 17

Don't watch too much tv

Boob tube, brain drain, idiot box—call it what you like. All these silly names do mean something. Think of all the time wasted by Americans who sit in front of the television watching brainless tv shows. Don't get me wrong, I love to relax in front of one great reality tv show, but that's all I need!

We Americans watch *way too much tv*! Children watch *way way too much tv*! Think of all the things we could be doing instead of letting our brain drain every night in front of the television. We could be playing board games and bonding with our families more often. We could be planning our next vacation! Perhaps we could be working on our new exciting business ventures that we want to tackle—dreaming big dreams and making big plans! We could be burning off that ice cream that we ate for dessert by going for a brisk walk, run or bike ride. It's a great time to get to know our spouses, children and friends better. How about reaching out to long-lost friends on the telephone, preparing our Christmas cards in September, making a fresh peach pie from scratch or fixing up our credit report?

Why should we be an audience to the American media and give them so much of our time and attention? What have they done for us lately? Our time is OUR time. It belongs to us. Let's not give it away so easily! Besides, wouldn't it be easier not to keep up with the Joneses if we didn't watch all the advertisements telling us how beautiful and popular we could be if we just bought their stuff?

By the way, I think it is crazy to watch the ten o'clock news. Can we have anything else more depressing on our minds when we go to sleep? I don't call it just the news—I call it the "bad news". Most of the news is negative and it puts our minds into a worried, sad and distressed state. If this is one of the last things we think about before bedtime, surely we will have negative thoughts and dreams as we sleep.

Tip # 18

Take time for Number One

We work, take care of our families, tend to our households, go to school and have so many responsibilities! Yes, a lot of these things would collapse without us. Or, at least, they wouldn't be as good. We spend so much time going, going, going that we forget about ourselves.

When I became a mom, I realized something no one told me: you have to be selfless. Everyone comes before me. That's just the way it is. But there is a balancing act to conquer!

Think about this for a minute:

Recall when the flight attendant tells us before we take off that we may need oxygen at some point during the flight. The mask will drop down from the ceiling and we are told to do what? Put the mask on you first and then help your children put on theirs. Do you apply that "command" to your life? If you are strong and secure and take care of yourself first, you will be in a much better position to care of others. Take time for yourself. Take care of your body, mind and spirit. The rest will come easily.

"In the event of a sudden loss of cabin pressure, oxygen masks will descend from the ceiling. Stop screaming, grab the mask, and pull it over your face. If you have a small child traveling with you, secure your mask before assisting with theirs. If you are traveling with two small children, decide now which one you love more."

~Airline employee

(Okay, Bad Mommy #2—I just couldn't resist!)

Tip # 19

Be all you can be

Did your parents tell you there is nothing you can't do? If not, then let me take the honor. *You can do anything you want to do!* If you believe you can, you can. And if you believe you can't, you can't. It starts with your thoughts and your beliefs. If you have "dream stealers" in your life, tell them to go steal someone else's dream. We live in America—the "land of opportunity". Immigrants have been coming in droves for centuries to have the "American Dream". It's right here, at your back door.

Start a business. Write a book. Play an instrument. Invest in real estate. Go back to school. Invent something and put it on the market. Learn to drive a motorcycle, scuba dive, or jump out of an airplane! You can achieve anything you set out to do. Don't try to keep up with the Joneses. Keep up with yourself and your unlimited possibilities! Don't let anyone get in your way. It's never too late!

"Keep away from people who try to belittle your ambitions. Small people always do that, but the really great make you feel that you, too, can become great."

~Mark Twain

Tip # 20

Take risks

Great risk equals great reward! It can also lead to failure. But if you never fail, you will never take any chances and, therefore, will never have great rewards. If status quo makes you happy, stay there. But if you want more out of life, you have to take risks. Oh, go ahead and spend a buck on the lottery every now and then!

"Anyone who has never made a mistake has never tried anything new"

~Albert Einstein

Tip # 21

Be adventurous

It's really safe and cheap to stay home and find a lot of things to keep you occupied. I know some people who prefer lying on the couch and reading about adventures but not living them. They have no plans to live them. Life is just fine on that big comfy couch, trying to experience things through colorful words in books.

Have you bought a book about "Things to See and Do" in your city or state? Do you try to uncover all the different places and experiences that you can? Imagine how educated you would be if you took every weekend and went somewhere in your town that you had never been before. (Of course you can, you live below your means, remember?)

When Michael and I married, I was new at my job and didn't have any vacation time. So, we got really creative and decided to see our local town through the eyes of a tourist! We stayed at one of the oldest hotels in downtown Ft. Lauderdale and enjoyed it immensely! We took a cruise on the Jungle Queen, which featured many sights that we had never seen before. I was ashamed because I had spent all of my life in this great town and never saw such things! We saw beautiful homes along the river (where the Joneses live!) and went to a small secluded area, where we ate barbeque and watched a Native Indian wrestle an alligator.

Later that day, we went shopping on Las Olas, a wonderful, chic, street in town with great boutiques and restaurants. We took a water taxi, which cruised down the Intracoastal Waterway, and dropped us off at restaurants and bars where we had never been. We had such a great time! We promised ourselves then that we would always live like tourists. We would see everything we could see and experience every adventure there is to have! We want to see and do everything that is available to us!

How many times have you said, "I really wanted to see that" or, "I have always wanted to go there"? Again, I say, "What are you waiting for?"

"A man's feet must be planted in his country, but his eyes should survey the world."

~George Santayana

Tip # 22

Live, love and dance

This is my theme! I have these words displayed all over my home. Live life like there's no tomorrow, love like you'll never get hurt and dance as if no one is watching! Make the best of life and every experience offered to you. Love people unconditionally, taking the best that they have to offer and dance wherever and whenever you darn-well please!

"The more you praise and celebrate your life, the more there is in life to celebrate."

~Oprah Winfrey

Tip # 23

Share

Did you ever read the book *All I Really Need to Know I Learned in Kindergarten by Robert Fulghum*? This lesson (share) was very important. I look at my life as being so full, abundant and blessed, that I want to share parts and pieces with others. One of my girlfriends said to me, "You have brought fun back into my life!" Wow, Can I really do that? Another friend says to me, "Well this person doesn't like this person because of this, so everyone else thinks this person is that", and so on and so on. Please! Let me just share my love with them—for who they are and for what they are to me! I want to believe that everyone is good and has so much love to reciprocate. Even if they don't, that's okay by me. At least I poured on the love as thick and as much as I could!

Have you ever seen a homeless person on the street? What do you do when they ask for a dollar? Have you thought about giving them twenty dollars? Think about what that will do for them. Better yet, what that will do for you? What about the bathroom attendant who has a meager jar of one dollar bills for all the good work they have done to fulfill the guests' needs? Have you ever plopped a five dollar bill in their lap? You'll never miss it *and* you will never forget the look of appreciation on their face. You may be the only person who ever thought enough to give them more than they expected. That small token could change their life forever!

"You can have everything in life that you want if you just give enough other people what they want."

~Zig Ziglar

Tip # 24

Be comfy in your skin

Have you seen the titles on the magazines that you find in line at the supermarket? If you haven't noticed, they are mostly about *losing weight* and *looking perfect*! How much money is this industry making every day? It seems that every single issue of every magazine I see has a blurb on the front page about "How to lose fifteen pounds in one month" or "How to have six pack abs in six weeks"! Please!

What is with this craze that you aren't good enough as you are physically?

Most people are not happy with their physical shape. Why? Because the media set the standard! The media shows us mostly perfect people and expects us to be just like them. By the way, here's a special lotion that you need to erase those wrinkles under your eyes and here's a special cream to remove the cellulite on your buttocks. There is no need to pay attention to all that hype. Happiness begins with you. It's believing in yourself and loving yourself like no one else. That's where it all begins. It matters so much more what is on the inside than what's on the outside.

All that said, what is really important is being healthy and staying healthy. How can you "Screw the Joneses" if you are too heavy to take a hike? It comes down to two simple things. You've heard it a million times but maybe this time will be the *call to action*. Eat healthy and exercise.

Everyone can *make a decision* to do these two simple things. If you do, you'll feel on top of the world. Eat a bowl of cereal in the morning, a salad for lunch and a piece of fish and some vegetables for dinner. Then—go for a walk (or "git' skinny" with a friend). Cut back on the snacking, drinking alcohol, and watching television. You'll be much better off! Why is it that Dr. "Imskinnierthanu" makes millions of dollars on his complicated diet when all you need are these two things? The best part is that it doesn't cost a bundle. Forget about all those silly diets that don't work!

Save your money. Eat smart and and take a hike! You can send me your money for that great diet advice, but I suggest putting the savings in your vacation fund!

Tip # 25

Git' skinny with your friends

Although it's important to be comfortable in your skin, there's nothing wrong with working toward being in good physical shape! My girlfriend and I go for walks and try to "git skinny" at least three times a week. We don't go to the expensive gyms (where you can find the Joneses); we simply walk around our neighborhood. We call it "gittin' skinny" because we are accomplishing two things at one time. We are exercising and burning calories, therefore, getting skinnier waistlines AND we are catching up with each other on our day and our experiences. We are, in essence, getting the "update" on each others' lives, which is better said … "Gittin' the skinny".

Gittin' skinny with a friend is fantastic! It's a great time to throw up all the garbage from the day and release it. At the same time, someone who loves you is listening and sharing advice or just saying, "It'll be ok!" Meanwhile, the calories are dropping off like hot butter! What a great way to end the day!

Tip # 26

Learn what a true friend really is

They say if you can count your friends on one hand, you are very blessed. I say that if you use more than one finger, you are one of the luckiest people in the world! It's very simple to figure out who your true friends really are. Ask yourself, "Who would pick me up from the airport at midnight?" or "who would come and take care of me if I was really sick?" and "Who can bring me up when I'm really feeling down?" If one of your friends consistently comes to mind after reading each of these questions, hold on tight! That person is GOLD! That person is a "true friend". Everyone else is a "friend".

True friends are non-judgmental. They will love you even if you don't drive a fancy car and have the name brand "things" that the Joneses have. They love you for you and not for your possessions. Treat your true friends the best you can and be thankful every day to have them in your life! Tell them you love them today. Don't wait until tomorrow!

> *"It's the friends you can call up at 4 a.m. that matter."*
>
> *~Marlene Dietrick*

Tip # 27

No doesn't always mean no

To me, the word 'no' means: not now, not in this particular place, at this particular time, with this particular person. That's all! Think of all the times someone told you "no" and that stopped you dead in your tracks. We are taught as children that "no means no". This *does not apply* to adults. We've earned our stripes as adults and have earned the right to deny a "No".

The founder of Kentucky Fried Chicken, **COLONEL SANDERS,** was told "No" one thousand and nine times before he sold his first piece of chicken. Sanders would drive from town to town, restaurant to restaurant, often sleeping in his car, living off his chicken and believing his "secret recipe" would one day pay off. Eventually his persistence and belief in himself paid off big time!

When **LUCILE BALL** (star of "I LOVE LUCY") began studying to be an actress in 1927, she was told by the head instructor of the John Murray Anderson Drama School, "Try any other profession. Any other."

After one of his first casting calls, this is what an MGM exec had to say about **FRED ASTAIRE:** "Can't sing. Balding. Can dance a little."

WALT DISNEY visited more than three hundred banks to get a loan and in 1955 his persistence paid off because he opened Disneyland in Anaheim, CA.

Did you know that it took **THOMAS EDISON** over nine thousand times before perfecting the light bulb?

"Great works are performed, not by strength, but by perseverance."

~Samuel Johnson

Don't Keep Up With the Joneses!

By the way, I love the Joneses! They keep us striving for better and aiming higher. They keep us on our toes and help us to not sit on our laurels and settle for mediocrity. I love the success stories we can learn from them and the advice they share quite openly. Without them, we'd be settling for much less in this great land of opportunity. So, I don't really mean Screw the Joneses. Kiss the Joneses and screw the "keep up with the Joneses" mentality!

"TO OVERCOME MONEY ENVY, WE NEED TO FIGURE OUT OUR PURPOSE, IDENTIFY WHAT WE LOVE AND VALUE MOST, AND MAKE OUR MONEY OBEY OUR VALUES BY SETTING SPECIFIC FINANCIAL GOALS. BECAUSE IF WE ACHIEVE THE THINGS WE VALUE MOST, WE'LL BE LESS RIVETED BY WHAT THE NEIGHBORS ARE DOING. THIS ISN'T A ONE-TIME EXERCISE, BUT A LIFELONG STRUGGLE. THE JONESES, THE MEDIA, AND AMERICAN CULTURE WILL FOREVER SEDUCE US TO BETRAY WHAT IS GENUINELY MEANINGFUL FOR WHAT IS COMFORTABLE, BEAUTIFUL, AND ENVIABLE."

~LAURA ROWLEY—YAHOO FINANCE

"A HUNDRED YEARS FROM NOW, IT WON'T MATTER WHAT KIND OF CAR I DROVE, THE KIND OF HOUSE I LIVED IN OR WHAT MY BANK ACCOUNT WAS. WHAT WILL MATTER IS THAT I MADE THE DIFFERENCE IN THE LIFE OF MY SPOUSE, MY CHILD, MY FAMILY, MY FRIENDS, PEOPLE IN NEED AND MYSELF!" IF YOU ASKED ME ON MY DEATHBED WHAT I WOULD DO DIFFERENTLY, I WOULD SAY, "ABSOLUTELY NOTHING! BUT MY ADVICE TO YOU, BABY, IS…. SCREW THE JONESES!"

~KRISTY FRANCES

Dear Reader,

Thank you for choosing and reading "Screw the Joneses!" This book was a lot of fun to write but we have only scratched the tip of the iceberg. There are so many other ways to screw the Joneses and have a blast while you last. Please visit our blog at our website www.screwthejoneses.com to share your creative thoughts and ideas on this subject. "Screw the Joneses" will be a series of books, compiling thoughts and suggestions from our readers. Help us to help our readers "de-Jones" their lives. If your comment is chosen and published, you will be given an official "Screw the Joneses" t-shirt. Also, please visit our website if you'd like to purchase our outrageous "Screw the Joneses" clothing and accessories.

978-0-595-46548-4
0-595-46548-X

Printed in the United States
137688LV00003B/5/A